SOME MAJOR EVENTS IN WORLD WAR II

THE EUROPEAN THEATER

1939 SEPTEMBER—Germany invades Poland; Great Britain, France, Australia, & New Zealand declare war on Germany; Battle of the Atlantic begins. NOVEMBER—Russia invades Finland.

1940 APRIL—Germany invades Denmark & Norway. MAY—Germany invades Belgium, Luxembourg, & The Netherlands; British forces retreat to Dunkirk and escape to England. JUNE—Italy declares war on Britain & France; France surrenders to Germany. JULY—Battle of Britain begins. SEPTEMBER—Italy invades Egypt; Germany, Italy, & Japan form the Axis countries. OCTOBER—Italy invades Greece. NOVEMBER—Battle of Britain over. DECEMBER—Britain attacks Italy in North Africa.

1941 JANUARY—Allies take Tobruk. FEBRUARY—Rommel arrives at Tripoli. APRIL—Germany invades Greece & Yugoslavia. JUNE—Allies are in Syria; Germany invades Russia. JULY—Russia joins Allies. AUGUST—Germans capture Kiev. OCTOBER—Germany reaches Moscow. DECEMBER—Germans retreat from Moscow; Japan attacks Pearl Harbor; United States enters war against Axis nations.

1942 MAY—first British bomber attack on Cologne. JUNE—Germans take Tobruk. SEPTEMBER—Battle of Stalingrad begins. OCTOBER—Battle of El Alamein begins. NOVEMBER—Allies recapture Tobruk; Russians counterattack at Stalingrad.

1943 JANUARY—Allies take Tripoli. FEBRUARY—German troops at Stalingrad surrender. APRIL—revolt of Warsaw Ghetto Jews begins. MAY—German and Italian resistance in North Africa is over; their troops surrender in Tunisia; Warsaw Ghetto revolt is put down by Germany. JULY—allies invade Sicily; Mussolini put in prison. SEPTEMBER—Allies land in Italy; Italians surrender; Germans occupy Rome; Mussolini rescued by Germany. OCTOBER—Allies capture Naples; Italy declares war on Germany. NOVEMBER—Russians recapture Kiev.

1944 JANUARY—Allies land at Anzio. JUNE—Rome falls to Allies; Allies land in Normandy (D-Day). JULY—assassination attempt on Hitler fails. AUGUST—Allies land in southern France. SEPTEMBER—Brussels freed. OCTOBER—Athens liberated. DECEMBER—Battle of the Bulge.

1945 JANUARY—Russians free Warsaw. FEBRUARY—Dresden bombed. APRIL—Americans take Belsen and Buchenwald concentration camps; Russians free Vienna; Russians take over Berlin; Mussolini killed; Hitler commits suicide. MAY—Germany surrenders; Goering captured.

THE PACIFIC THEATER

1940 SEPTEMBER—Japan joins Axis nations Germany & Italy.

1941 APRIL—Russia & Japan sign neutrality pact. DECEMBER—Japanese launch attacks against Pearl Harbor, Hong Kong, the Philippines, & Malaya; United States and Allied nations declare war on Japan; China declares war on Japan, Germany, & Italy; Japan takes over Guam, Wake Island, & Hong Kong; Japan attacks Burma.

1942 JANUARY—Japan takes over Manila; Japan invades Dutch East Indies. FEBRUARY—Japan takes over Singapore; Battle of the Java Sea. APRIL—Japanese overrun Bataan. MAY—Japan takes Mandalay; Allied forces in Philippines surrender to Japan; Japan takes Corregidor; Battle of the Coral Sea. JUNE—Battle of Midway; Japan occupies Aleutian Islands. AUGUST—United States invades Guadalcanal in the Solomon Islands.

1943 FEBRUARY—Guadalcanal taken by U.S. Marines. MARCH—Japanese begin to retreat in China. APRIL—Yamamoto shot down by U.S. Air Force. MAY—U.S. troops take Aleutian Islands back from Japan. JUNE—Allied troops land in New Guinea. NOVEMBER—U.S. Marines invade Bougainville & Tarawa.

1944 FEBRUARY—Truk liberated. JUNE—Saipan attacked by United States. JULY—battle for Guam begins. OCTOBER—U.S. troops invade Philippines; Battle of Leyte Gulf won by Allies.

1945 JANUARY—Luzon taken; Burma Road won back. MARCH—Iwo Jima freed. APRIL—Okinawa attacked by U.S. troops; President Franklin Roosevelt dies; Harry S. Truman becomes president. JUNE—United States takes Okinawa. AUGUST—atomic bomb dropped on Hiroshima; Russia declares war on Japan; atomic bomb dropped on Nagasaki. SEPTEMBER—Japan surrenders.

WORLD AT WAR

Death of Hitler

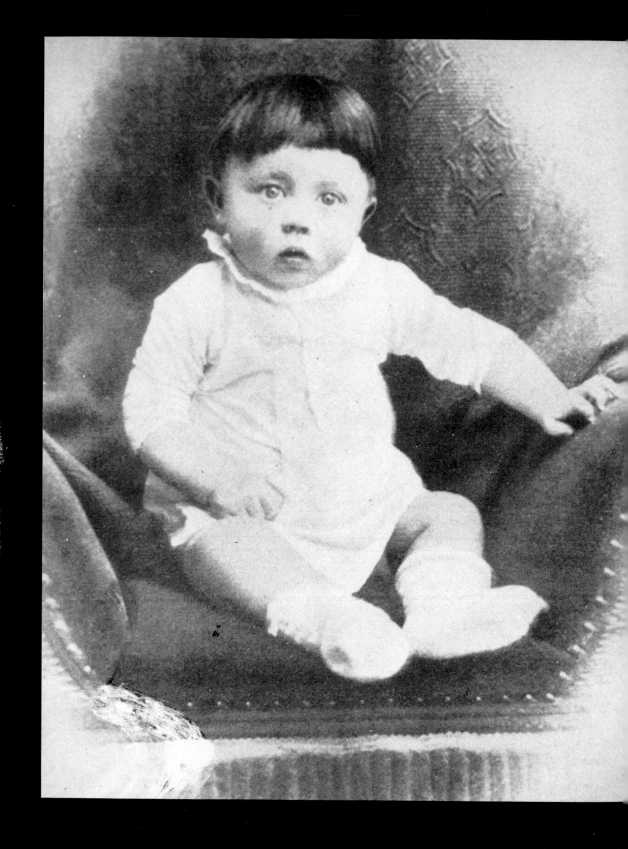

WORLD AT WAR

Death of Hitler

By G.C. Skipper

Consultant:
Professor Robert L. Messer, Ph.D.
Department of History
University of Illinois at Chicago Circle

CHILDRENS PRESS ™

CHICAGO

The elegant cabinet room in the Reich Chancellery before being destroyed by bombs and artillery shells.

FRONTISPIECE:
Baby picture of Adolf Hitler

Library of Congress Cataloging in Publication Data
Skipper, G.C.
  The death of Hitler.

  (His World at war)
  SUMMARY: Describes events in the last days of Adolf Hitler before he committed suicide in a bunker during the Russian shelling of Berlin.
  1. Hitler, Adolf, 1889-1945—Death and burial —Juvenile literature. 2. Heads of state— Germany—Biography—Juvenile literature. [1. Hitler, Adolf, 1889-1945—Death and burial. 2. Heads of state] I. Title. II. Series.
DD247. H58S54 943.086'092'4 [B] [92] 80-17180
ISBN 0-516-04783-3

PROJECT EDITOR:
Joan Downing

CREATIVE DIRECTOR:
Margrit Fiddle

PICTURE CREDITS:
U.S. ARMY PHOTOGRAPH: Cover, pages 8 (bottom), 13, 18, 20 (bottom right), 21,23 (bottom), 33, 34, 35, 37, 38, 41, 45 (top left and bottom), 46
UPI: pages 4, 15, 17 (bottom), 20 (bottom left), 22, 28, 31 (top right), 39, 43, 45 (top right)
NATIONAL ARCHIVES: pages 6, 8 (top), 17 (top), 20 (top), 23 (top), 31 (top left and bottom)
U.S. AIR FORCE PHOTO: pages 25, 27
LEN MEENTS (map): page 11

COVER PHOTO:
"Heil Hitler!" is a photo from Eva Braun's collection

The two members of the Nazi High Command sat outside the war room. They were waiting to be called.

"Won't they ever *stop*?" The one who had spoken kept his voice low. But fear and frustration could be heard in his voice.

"Keep quiet," his companion told him, "or we'll both be shot for treason."

They were waiting down below in the bunker. But still they could hear the artillery shells. The explosions above them made the entire earth tremble. The shelling seemed endless.

"The Russians are at the very gates of Berlin!" the Nazi officer said. "Doesn't Hitler know that?"

Suddenly another shell landed. The bunker shook so badly that the officer dropped his briefcase to the ground. "This is insanity!" he said. When he picked up the briefcase his hands trembled.

"I said keep quiet!" his companion said. "He is still *Der Fuehrer* (the Leader)."

The Nazi officer settled the briefcase on his lap.
He stared upward at the roof of the bunker. At one
time, up there, had stood the Reich Chancellery. Its
marble walls rose toward the sky. Its huge wooden
doors opened on a powerful city. The Reich
Chancellery had been a grand building. It had been
the seat of German power. It had caused pride in
those who wore the swastika arm bands and the tall
jackboots. Now the officer wondered what had
gone wrong.

It was April 1945. The Reich Chancellery was
not much more than a shell. It had been badly
damaged by repeated bombings. Sections of the
outer walls were gone. Artillery shells had been
lobbed into the very yard of the Chancellery. They
had ripped out huge craters. The air was filled with
smoke and rock dust. Inside the building, marble
walls were broken. Only bits and blasted pieces of
once-lavish chandeliers hung from crumbling
ceilings. Plaster dust coated everything.

Now we are like rats, thought the Nazi officer, living below ground in a bunker. The bunker was a maze of tunnels and rooms beneath the Chancellery. There, the few members of the Nazi inner circle lived and worked. There they were protected. But the bunker was no longer safe. Soon the Russians would be there. And still Hitler would not admit that Germany had lost World War II.

"If the artillery would only stop," the Nazi officer said again. "I no longer can hear my own thoughts."

"That is probably best," his companion answered.

To gain control of himself, the officer took the papers out of the briefcase. He looked at them closely. The German armies in the west had launched the Ardennes counter offensive. But the attack had failed. The Allied Army had destroyed the Germans.

The officer flipped the pages of the report. The Nazi division in the east had failed to stop the

Baltic Sea

North Sea

HAMBURG

Elbe River

Oder
River

GERMANY
1945

BREMEN

BERLIN

AMSTERDAM

HANNOVER

Spree R.

NETHERLANDS

ROTTERDAM

DORTMUND

LEIPZIG

Neisse
River

GERMANY

BRUSSELS

DÜSSELDORF

BELGIUM

Rhine River

FRANKFURT

PRAGUE

CZECHOSLOVAKIA

NUREMBERG

LUXEMBOURG

Danube River

MUNICH

Russians. The truth was, the officer realized at once, that Germany was nearly cut in two. The Americans had already crossed the Elbe River. The Russians had crossed the Oder and Neisse.

The officer shivered. The Russians were almost in Berlin. In a very short time the Russians and the Americans would meet. Germany was destroyed—and with it the powerful Third Reich. "We must convince him to leave, to go south for his own safety," the Nazi officer said.

"Adolf Hitler will never leave Berlin," said his companion. "You know that as well as I do."

"Then are we to die with him? Are we to just sit here and wait?" the officer said. His voice was louder than he intended. "Do you know what will happen to us when the Russians discover the bunker?" There was fear in the officer's eyes. "Think about it! Are you ready for that?"

"We can't run away! That is desertion!"

The officer put the papers back into the briefcase. Very calmly he handed the briefcase to his companion. "There is nothing to desert from, don't you see? There is no German army left. There is no German air force. No German navy. There is no Reich Chancellery. There is no Third Reich."

"But there *is* Adolf Hitler," his companion said. He looked over his shoulder to see if anyone else had entered the corridor of the bunker. It was empty. The door to the war room was still closed.

"Did you not hear what happened with the *Leibstandarte Adolf Hitler*? You know how they were.

A grim-faced Adolf Hitler surveys the ravages of war in Germany during the days before he buried himself in the bunker under the Reich Chancellery.

They believed Hitler's word was sacred. They never questioned his orders. They were the elite, remember? Yet when they were overwhelmed in the Upper Danube, what happened?"

"I do not wish to discuss it," his companion said.

"You know very well what happened. Hitler went into a rage. He denounced all of them—although they were fighting against impossible odds on his orders. He even demanded that they rip off their arm bands!"

"I suggest you let the matter alone," his companion warned.

The Nazi officer ignored him and went on talking. "They sent Hitler the arm bands as he requested—in a chamber pot! I was there, I tell you! One of the arm bands was still on the severed arm of a dead soldier!"

"Shut up!" his companion shouted.

At that moment, another artillery shell fell in the Chancellery yard above. The bunker trembled under the pounding. The explosions drowned out the voices of the two Nazis. Suddenly, the officer sprang to his feet.

"I will not wait for the Russians!" he said and ran toward the exit.

"Hans, wait!" his companion cried, standing up. But the officer had already disappeared. The remaining officer gripped the briefcase tightly. He stared down the empty corridor. "Fool!" he said to himself. "They will shoot you for that."

Without warning, the door to the war room opened. Another Nazi officer stood at the entrance.

Hitler and Jodl examine a huge map spread out on an oaken table.

"We are ready to start." the officer said. "Please come in. Where is Hans?"

For a moment the Nazi with the briefcase said nothing. Then he replied, "I don't know. He is not here."

"Well, let's get on with it. Move along, *Der Fuehrer* is waiting."

Inside the conference room lights burned brightly. A huge map was spread on a large oaken table. Several officers were already there, bending over the maps. Others stood about the room, waiting patiently. In a far corner stood Josef

Goebbels, the Propaganda Minister. Goebbels had abandoned his desire to be a writer and had pledged his entire allegiance to Adolf Hitler. Goebbels worshipped Hitler.

Goebbels was a small man with a club foot. Yet his physical defect took nothing away from his mastery of words and his power. Goebbels did not look very happy.

Standing almost unnoticed along the far wall was Martin Bormann. Everyone kept away from Bormann. He was constantly at Hitler's elbow.

As the Nazi with the briefcase sat down, he scanned the room. Familiar faces surrounded him. Men stood about, waiting, talking quietly in tiny circles. Goebbels, Keitel, Bormann, Jodl.

Two faces were missing. Heinrich Himmler, head of the SS— and probably the most feared man in the Nazi party—was nowhere to be seen. Even the thought of Himmler's name made the Nazi with the briefcase nervous.

Martin Bormann (left) was present at the April 22 conference.

Hermann Goering (below with Hitler) did not attend.

Also missing was Hermann Goering, head of the now non-existant Luftwaffe, the Nazi air force. He was a huge, fat man who looked foolish in the high jackboots and tight pants. Sometimes he wore a light, full uniform which made him look like the billowing sails of a big ship.

Hitler's 1943 birthday party (above) was a happier occasion than the birthday in 1945.

Though the officer didn't know it, both men had left Berlin two days earlier. They had stayed for Hitler's birthday party on April 20. They had stayed for the military conference afterward. Then they had left the threatened city.

For a moment the officer wished he had listened to Hans. He, too, should have left the bunker. It seemed as if everything around him was unreal. A group of madmen were playing war games.

Then Adolf Hitler entered the room. Immediately the entire High Command came to attention. In one voice, those in the room said, "Heil Hitler!" Their arms were outstretched stiffly. Their palms were down.

Hitler was deathly pale. He was trembling. As he made his way toward his chair, his left leg dragged. He was stooped over. He looked like an old man, yet he wasn't. Only two days earlier he had celebrated his fifty-sixth birthday.

The Nazi with the briefcase was shocked. He had seen Hitler at each daily conference. But now it was as if he were seeing Hitler for the first time—really seeing him.

It was hard to believe that this trembling, tired man was the same as the Hitler of earlier and better days. Then he had stood proudly before thousands of admiring Germans. He had promised them the Third Reich would live for a thousand years. That man had stood behind the podium and

whipped the crowds into frenzied excitement. He
was a far cry from the man the Nazi officer saw
before him now.

That other Adolf Hitler had stood with
outstretched hand, smiling. His black moustache
had been clipped to a neat square. His black hair
had slanted across his brow. Back then his eyes had
flashed brilliantly as he accepted the adoration of
his fanatic followers.

Instead of a thousand years of power, Adolf
Hitler had led them into a fiery hell of war and
defeat. Instead of delivering glory and victory, he
had crushed innocent nations with his once-mighty
armies. He had murdered innocent men, women,
and children behind the terrible walls of
concentration camps. Instead of pride, he had
delivered shame. He intended that every Jew in
Europe would be exterminated. Only the master
Aryan race was to survive and rule in racial purity.
Adolf Hitler had come very close to conquering the
world.

Above: Nazis try to keep people from buying goods from a Jewish merchant. Boycotts were among the early steps the Nazis took to eliminate Jews from Germany.
Below: Hitler with enthusiastic members of the "master Aryan race" in Graz, Austria.

Now he trembled and dragged himself across the room.

"First," Hitler said, "I will hear the reports from the front. I especially want to hear how Steiner is doing."

Keitel and Jodl looked at each other. They didn't know what to say. The day before, Hitler had ordered a counterattack on the Russians, who were already on the outskirts of Berlin. He had demanded that General Steiner gather all the soldiers in Berlin for the attack. The Steiner army was to push the Russians back and keep them back. Hitler was determined to keep Berlin safe.

But Hitler had lost touch with reality. There weren't enough troops in Berlin for such a counterattack. No one had had the nerve to point this out to Hitler. And now no one at the conference knew what to say. There had been no attempt to attack the Russians. No one knew where Steiner and his "army" were.

This aerial photo of Berlin was taken in May, 1944, during one of the many bombing raids by the United States Air Force.

But the war leaders did brief Hitler on the other battles. Without exception, the reports were bad. The ministers tried to cover up the truth of the defeats. But there seemed to be nothing but bad news from all fronts.

Hitler listened without a word. He tried to hide his left arm, which was trembling. The briefing dragged on. Time seemed to crawl. The weary voices droned on and on. Artillery shells continued to explode above the bunker.

Suddenly, Hitler lost control. He pounded his right fist down on the table. The loud *whack* startled those in the room. He shouted at the top of his voice: "You speak only of defeat! That is all I have heard from each of you. Defeat! Everyone has deceived me! No one has told me the truth! We shall never give up! Never!"

Suddenly Hitler slumped down in his chair, exhausted. "The Third Reich has failed," he said. The words were spoken softly. "There is nothing left to do but stay here and die with Berlin. That is my decision. I will stay in Berlin and die!" He immediately dictated an announcement to a secretary. Goebbels would read it over the radio that evening. Then the world would know that *Der Fuehrer* planned to defend Berlin to the end.

Wearily, Hitler raised his hand and dismissed the men. He would not listen to their protests. It was April 22, 1945. This was the last conference Hitler held with his war leaders.

As the Nazi with the briefcase left the room, he looked back. Hitler was a broken man. He was slumped in the chair behind the table. He is insane, the Nazi thought. Hans was right. There is nothing left but to stay alive.

Quickly he left the bunker. He was already planning how he would make his escape toward the American troops. If he could reach the Americans he would surrender.

The next morning Adolf Hitler felt much better.
He was in a good mood, in high spirits. His
depression was gone. Now he felt good. Once
again, he was convinced that the Third Reich was
destined for victory. Those other idiots had no faith,
he told himself. What would happen to all of them
if I showed such weakness? The very thought made
him smile. Yes, Hitler thought, victory will be ours.
I was called to lead the German people to victory. I
am not like the others.

Hitler was finishing lunch when an aide suddenly rushed into the room. Hitler looked up. He seemed relaxed. "What is it?" he asked.

"A telegram, Mein Fuehrer," the aide told him, "from Hermann Goering."

Hitler opened the telegram and began to read:

"In view of your decision to remain in the fortress of Berlin, do you agree that I take over at once the total leadership of the Reich...."

Hitler was furious. "Traitor!" he screamed. "That drug addict! Imbecile!" He went into a rage. He stormed and shouted and yelled for an aide. Pacing back and forth, he dictated a telegram in response to Goering's wire.

"Tell that drug-addicted imbecile that he is guilty of high treason," Hitler said. "Tell him he should be shot! Tell him, however, that because of his outstanding service in the past—a record I cannot ignore—he will not receive the ultimate punishment—death. I will let him keep his life, but he is to resign all his offices—at once!"

"Is that all, Mein Fuehrer?" the aide asked.

"Get out of here!" Hitler shouted. "Get out of my sight!" He slumped down in his chair.

The days dragged on. One disaster after another befell Germany. Hitler sat through the minutes and the hours and the days. He spent his time talking with his close associates—his doctor, his secretaries, and Eva Braun, his girl friend.

Much of his conversation was about the past. During one of these conversations Hitler began talking about an assassination attempt made against him. "Nine months ago a group of Nazi officers tried to assassinate me. A bomb carried in a briefcase exploded at a military conference. As you all know, that attempt failed. The guilty officers were punished. Severely punished."

"Fate intended me to lead the Fatherland to victory or I would not have survived that foul attempt on my life. But I did survive. And I had faith that a miracle would take place to deliver our troops into victory."

During the last days in the bunker, Hitler spent much time thinking about his triumphs of the past. In 1924, while in Landsberg prison (above left), he wrote his book *Mein Kampf* (My Struggle). In it he spelled out his beliefs and his plans for the future of Germany. In 1930 (above right) he is shown wearing the Nazi brown shirt during the time he was building the Nazi party. He was named chancellor of Germany in 1933 (below), and very soon afterward became a dictator.

"When the evil leader of the United States—Roosevelt—died, I believed that was the miracle we had been waiting for. I still believe that. It is only a matter of time before the alliance between the United States and Britain and Russia falls apart. It is already beginning to happen."

Suddenly Hitler's voice rose to an angry screech. "No one else has any faith. No one else believes!"

He lectured his friends for hours on end. He talked of his philosophy, his political beliefs, and the war. He told them how the tide of war would change and that Germany would be victorious. He often compared himself to Alexander the Great. There were long, endless dinners reaching into the early morning hours.

Hitler talked constantly. His moods changed often. But most of his talk was a boring monologue. Often his inner circle members fell asleep at the table. No matter how hard they tried, it was hard to stay awake. They would awaken suddenly, afraid Hitler had noticed their dozing. They feared his outrages.

Even before he had Blondi, Hitler usually had a dog nearby.

The only member of the inner circle who seemed contented was Hitler's favorite dog, Blondi. The animal stayed with his master. He never questioned. He was never aware that anything was wrong. One of the few times Hitler's face softened was when he looked down at the dog. He would nearly smile as he rubbed the dog gently behind the ears.

Exploding shells were a menace to both Allied and Axis troops in Berlin.

Meanwhile, above the bunker, the Russians were closing in. Artillery shells were exploding more and more furiously every day.

On the evening of April 28, a news broadcast was heard in the bunker. Heinrich Himmler had tried to begin peace negotiations with the Allies. Even now he was in Lubeck talking to Count Bernadotte.

Hitler was furious. He ranted and raged. He prowled up and down the corridors of the bunker. He shouted at everyone he saw. "Treason! Himmler! Himmler!" he yelled. "Himmler— against my direct orders, without my knowledge— tried to negotiate a peace settlement! Those negotiations have failed! I will consent to no peace! Only German victory!"

Suddenly the outburst was over. Hitler's mood changed. His shoulders slumped. "Nothing now remains. Nothing is spared me," he said. "No loyalty is kept, no honor observed. There is no bitterness, no betrayal that has not yet been heaped upon me."

On April 28, 1945, Hitler called in his secretaries. He dictated two documents. One was his personal will. The other summed up his political beliefs. It also laid out the lines of succession. He made very clear who he wanted as his successor. He also made very clear just how the new government should be set up. He had learned

An early picture of Eva Braun

nothing from defeat. He had learned nothing from his mistakes. He blamed everyone but himself for the collapse of the Third Reich.

That same day, Hitler told his associates that he was to be married. He and Eva Braun were, in fact, to be married that very day.

There was a strange kind of excitement in the bunker that day. Hitler received congratulations from all those present. Yet part of his will read: "I myself and my wife—in order to escape the disgrace of overthrow or capitulation—choose death."

Feelings were mixed throughout the bunker. Hitler's followers were overjoyed by the news that their leader had planned his wedding day. Yet, above them, Germany was falling apart. They also knew that Hitler did not intend to leave the bunker alive. Many of them were already thinking of their own escape from the madness that surrounded them.

One of the last things Adolf Hitler did during his remaining hours on earth was to marry Eva Braun. After the wedding there was a celebration in the bunker. Hitler and his new bride stayed with the wedding party for a while. Then in the small hours of the morning, they disappeared into Hitler's suite.

When Hitler and Eva left the room, it was as if a great burden had been lifted from the shoulders of the people who were in the inner circle. They drank and laughed and danced—something they would never have done before, not with Hitler nearby.

Now it did not matter anymore. For a moment they forgot their fear. The party became so loud,

finally, that word was sent from Hitler's suite of
eighteen rooms to keep the noise down.

It was a strange chain of events that led closer
and closer to the end of the Third Reich. The men
and women left in the bunker no longer seemed
able to tell fantasy from reality, good from evil.

The next morning—April 30, 1945—the newly married Adolf Hitler arose at his usual hour. He had breakfast and went about the routine matters of the day. At lunch, however, the routine was broken.

He had his meal, as usual, but after lunch Hitler reached down and fondly patted his dog, Blondi, for the last time. He issued an order and the dog was taken away and killed.

Pale, trembling, his eyes staring into space as if he were looking at something beyond all of them, Hitler visited the people left in the bunker. He shook hands and said good-bye. Some of the women wept.

Josef Goebbels, for the first time in his life, refused to obey a direct order from Hitler. He flatly rejected Hitler's order for him to take his family and leave the bunker for safety. Goebbels said he and his wife and his children would remain and die in the bunker with Hitler. He was true to his word.

After saying farewell, Hitler returned with Eva Braun to his suite of rooms. For a while no one

Hitler poses with Magda and Josef Goebbels and three of the six Goebbels children.

seemed to know what to do. Some already were making frantic attempts to get out of the bunker while they could. The explosions above seemed to be getting worse. Others just stood around, at a loss.

Then, at 3:15 P.M., a single shot echoed through the corridors of the bunker. For a moment no one moved. No one spoke. Suddenly two members of the Nazi inner circle rushed into Hitler's room.

Adolf Hitler was on a blood-soaked sofa. He had shot himself. Nearby Eva Braun lay dead. She had taken poison.

"My God, what do we do now?" one of the Nazis asked. He looked shocked. The other was quite calm.

"We carry out the final orders of *Der Fuehrer*," the other Nazi said.

The bodies were carried from the bunker out into the sunlight of the yard. Amid falling artillery shells and dangerous explosions, the bodies were soaked with gasoline and burned.

One of the most powerful—and evil—leaders of World War II was dead.

His dream of racial purity and world domination died with him. The only thing that did not die with Adolf Hitler was the memory of the unspeakable murders and senseless tortures he inflicted on millions of innocent people.

But even in that memory it is not Adolf Hitler who is remembered—but his victims.

The end of the Third Reich.
Above: An American GI looks at the shallow ditch in the rubble of the Reich Chancellery where the bodies of the Hitlers were burned. Below: German military heads Stumpf, Keitel, and Friedeburg not long before Jodl and Friedeburg signed the surrender for Germany on May 7, 1945. Left: President Harry S. Truman (in white hat and dark suit) views the Reich Chancellery at war's end.

INDEX

*Page numbers in boldface type
indicate illustrations*

About the Author

A native of Alabama, G.C. Skipper has traveled throughout the world, including Jamaica, Haiti, India, Argentina, the Bahamas, and Mexico. He has written several other children's books as well as an adult novel. Mr. Skipper has also published numerous articles in national magazines. He is now working on his second adult novel. Mr. Skipper and his family live in North Wales, Pennsylvania, a suburb of Philadelphia.